The Magic of Kol Nidre

A YOM KIPPUR STORY

Bruce H. Siegel

illustrations by Shelly O. Haas

KAR-BEN COPIES, INC. ROCKVILLE, MD

This story is dedicated to my beloved grandfather
Charles Abraham Rovner ז״ל
who kept me from getting lost in the prayerbook,
and to my sweet Anne
who keeps me from getting lost now.
— BHS

In loving memory of my Grandpa Mazzucchi.
Special thanks to Rabbis James Friedman and Jacob Izakson,
also to Anna, Robert, Dillon, Michael, Julie, Abigayil and Geoffrey.
—SOH

Library of Congress Cataloging-in-Publication Data

Siegel, Bruce H.
    The Magic of Kol Nidre: A Story for Yom Kippur / Bruce H. Siegel
: illustrated by Shelly O. Haas.
        p.   cm.
    Summary: The magic of the Kol Nidre prayer, central to the Yom Kippur service,
is explored from the viewpoint of three generations.
    ISBN 1-58013-003-8 (hc). — ISBN 1-58013-002-X (pbk).
    1. Kol Nidrei — Juvenile literature. 2. Yom Kippur — Juvenile literature.
(1. Kol Nidrei. 2. Yom Kippur) I. Haas, Shelly O., ill. II. Title
296.4'532—DC21
                                                                97-19314
                                                                    CIP
                                                                    AC

Published by KAR-BEN COPIES, INC., Rockville, MD 1-800-4-KARBEN
Printed in the United States of America

FOREWORD

Yom Kippur, the Day of Atonement, is the holiest day in the Jewish year. It is a day of forgiveness and repentance, when Jews the world over come to synagogue to make peace with God and with themselves.

The preface to the Yom Kippur prayers is the chanting of Kol Nidre on the eve of the holiday. The cantor and two witnesses constitute a beit din, or court of law, with the power to annul vows made to God. Because it is a legal proceeding, it must begin before sundown, and the declaration is recited three times for emphasis. Traditionally the cantor begins Kol Nidre softly and sings it louder each time.

Over the centuries other reasons have been given for singing Kol Nidre three times. The Maharal (Chief Rabbi of Prague in the 17th century) said it is to intensify the mood of awe and prayer. According to the Machzor Vitri (an 11th century legal-liturgical work based on the scholarship of the great commentator Rashi), "The first time the reader must utter it very softly, like one who hesitates to enter the palace of a king to ask for a gift; the second time he may speak louder; and the third time more loudly still, as one who is accustomed to dwell at the court and to approach the ruler as a friend."

One Yom Kippur eve, when I was very young, my grandfather took me to the synagogue. I had never seen so many people there before. Every seat was taken, and people were standing in the back. As we waited for the cantor to begin, my grandfather quietly turned the pages in his prayerbook humming the familiar passages, and I played with the fringes of his long, white tallit, winding the strands around my fingers.

"Why have all these people come?" I asked.

"They have come to hear the cantor sing *Kol Nidre*," he answered.

"Is it very beautiful?" I asked.

"Yes," he said. "And sad."

"Is it long?" I asked.

"No. But it is important. *Kol Nidre* asks forgiveness for promises we may make to God which we may not be able to keep."

"Is it the most important prayer?"

My grandfather thought a moment. "No, but when *Kol Nidre* is sung there is magic."

"Magic!" my mouth and eyes opened wide.

"Not the magic of rabbits in hats, or things disappearing and reappearing," he answered. "It is a special magic. And for the magic to happen, the cantor must sing the prayer three times — once very softly, once somewhat louder, and the third time more loudly still."

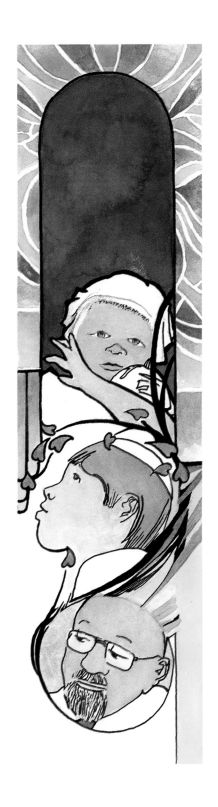

"I know!" I exclaimed. "The cantor sings softly for babies who get frightened by loud noises. He sings in his usual voice for people who have good ears. And he sings loudly for people who can't hear very well."

"That's a good answer," my grandfather said, gently touching the end of my nose with his soft, leathery finger. "But one day you may have an even better one."

"But..." I began, as he shushed me and motioned that we should stand.

The rabbi rose from a big chair on the bimah and asked that the doors be closed. No one was to enter or leave while *Kol Nidre* was being sung. The ark was opened. Leaders of the congregation removed two Torah scrolls and stood on either side of the podium. The cantor took his place between them. He paused for a very long time, and began to sing.

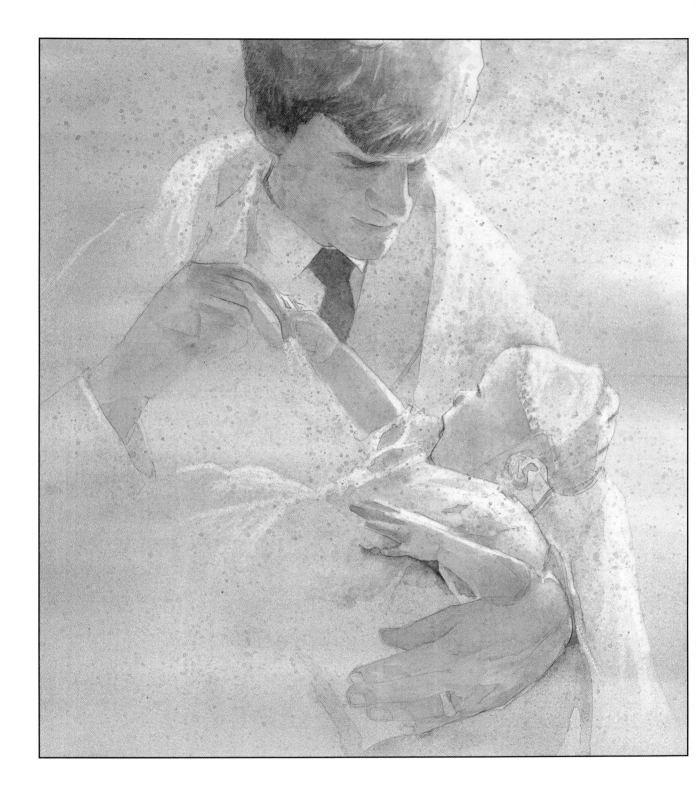

Years later, on another Yom Kippur eve, my wife and I sat in the synagogue waiting for *Kol Nidre* to begin. I was holding our new baby. We sat near the door, so that if she started to cry, I could take her outside into the hall. I dangled one of the fringes of my tallit just above her nose, and, as she reached upward with her pudgy hands, I thought of my grandfather. She was named for him.

I remember being disappointed that I had seen no magic. "For the magic to happen, *Kol Nidre* must be sung three times," he said. I still wasn't sure why, although I was older, and, I hoped, smarter than when I'd sat beside him those many years ago.

A few rows in front of us an old man was dozing. I smiled and thought to myself, "We sing *Kol Nidre* once quietly for those who are paying attention, once a little louder for those whose minds are wandering, and once loudly to wake those who have fallen asleep."

My little daughter managed to grab hold of the fringe and gurgled happily. Without thinking I touched a finger to the tip of her nose. "Maybe there will be magic tonight, sweetheart," I said softly.

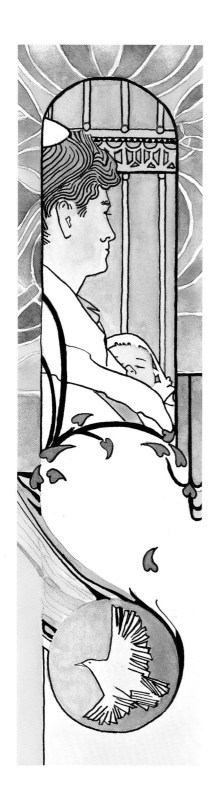

The rabbi rose from a big chair on the bimah and asked that the doors be closed. No one was to enter or leave while *Kol Nidre* was being sung. The ark was opened. Leaders of the congregation removed two Torah scrolls and stood on either side of the podium. The cantor took his place between them. He paused for a very long time, and began to sing.

It is the eve of yet another Yom Kippur. I squint through my glasses trying to see the letters in the prayer book more clearly. My grandson, who is six, leans against me on the pew and plays with my tallit, winding the strands around his little fingers.

"When will they start, Grandpa?" he asks impatiently.

"Soon." I answer him. "The cantor is getting ready to sing *Kol Nidre*."

"I know all about that," my grandson says with authority. "We learned about it in Sunday School."

"And did you learn about the magic that happens when the cantor sings *Kol Nidre*? Or why he must sing it three times?"

"What magic?" he asks.

I look at the people milling around the sanctuary and know that finally I understand the magic of *Kol Nidre*. All these years, the answer was around me and I didn't see it.

It is the people. The people who every year on Yom Kippur fill the synagogues of the world to hear a simple, sad melody sung in a language most of them hardly know. Still they come, often not knowing why. Not understanding what draws them. Knowing only that this is what Jews do. Religious Jews and Jews who don't believe. Jews who come to synagogue every week, and Jews who come but once a year. Jews for whom the holidays are a joy, and Jews for whom the holidays are a mystery.

"So what about the magic?" he persists.

"That," I say, touching the tip of his nose with my finger, " is something you will discover for yourself by coming to hear *Kol Nidre* every year. But I can tell you why I think it is sung three times," I say.

"First, the cantor sings it very softly for our ancestors, our fathers and mothers and grandfathers and grandmothers, all those who have come before us and whom we have loved. For those whose lives we hold in our memories, a soft *Kol Nidre* will do.

"Then he sings the prayer a little louder. This time it's for you and me. He doesn't sing too softly because my ears are old and don't hear too well. And he doesn't sing too loudly because your ears are young and sharp.

"Finally, when he sings *Kol Nidre* the third time, he sings as loud as he can, so that your children and your grandchildren, and all the children yet to be born can hear it."

My grandson looks up at me, his eyes wide. His fingers have stopped playing with my fringes.

The rabbi rises from a big chair on the bimah and asks that the doors be closed. No one is to enter or leave while *Kol Nidre* is being sung. The ark is opened. Leaders of the congregation remove two Torah scrolls and stand on either side of the podium. The cantor takes his place between them. He pauses for a very long time, and begins to sing.

ABOUT THE AUTHOR

Cantor Bruce Siegel and his wife Anne live in Savannah, GA, where he is the cantor for Congregations Mickve Israel and Agudath Achim and the Education Director for the Shalom School. He has published a college radio production textbook and three other stories for children. The Siegels' son, Joshua, is an artist living in New York City.

ABOUT THE ILLUSTRATOR

Shelly O. Haas was raised in a home where the arts were very important. She earned a BFA in Illustration from the Rhode Island School of Design. Shelly has illustrated seven books for Kar-Ben, including *Daddy's Chair,* winner of the 1992 Sydney Taylor Award from the Assocation of Jewish Libraries, and *Thank You, God,* a 1993 National Jewish Book Awards Honor Book.